DATE DUE

The Butterfly in the Sky

by **Dana Meachen Rau**

Reading Consultant: Nanci R. Vargus, Ed. D.

Marshall Cavendish
Benchmark
New York

Picture Words

birds

branch

butterfly

caterpillar

's caterpillar's

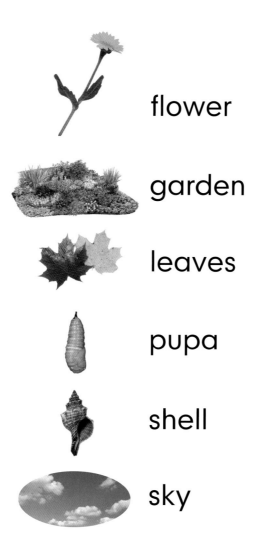

flower

garden

leaves

pupa

shell

sky

3

Munch, munch, munch.

A  eats .

The 's legs help it climb.

Its legs help it hold on to 🍁.

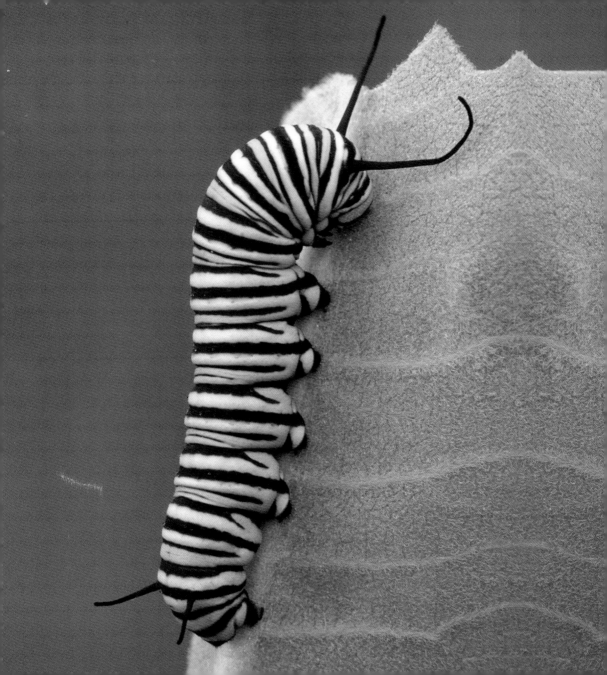

The  is ready
to rest.

It finds a spot on
a 🪵.

The 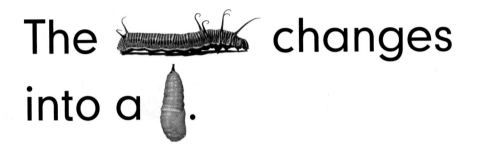 changes into a .

The is hard, like a .

In two weeks a 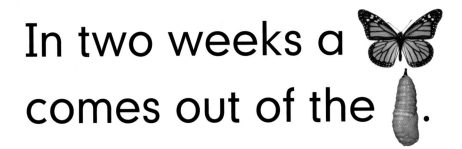 comes out of the 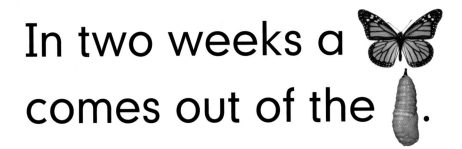.

The 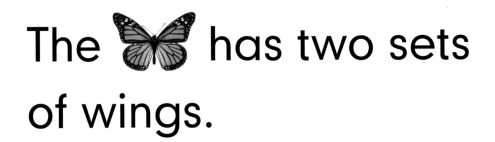 has two sets of wings.

The  flies in the to the .

The  looks out for hungry .

The  lands on a .

The sucks the

nectar.

The 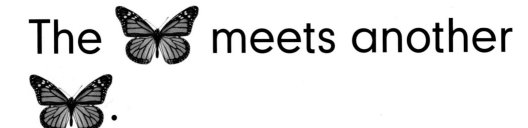 meets another
.

Next the lays eggs.

Then a  comes out of an egg.

The  is ready to eat.

Munch, munch, munch.

Words to Know

climb (klime)
      to crawl up

hungry (HUHNG-ree)
      to want food

munch (muhnch)
      to chew

nectar (NEK-tur)
      a sweet juice in flowers

Find Out More

Books

Ehlert, Lois. *Waiting for Wings*. San Diego, CA:
Harcourt Children's Books, 2001.

Lerner, Carol. *Butterflies in the Garden*. New York:
HarperCollins, 2002.

Rockwell, Anne F. *Becoming Butterflies*.
New York: Walker and Company, 2002.

Zemlicka, Shannon. *From Egg to Butterfly*.
Minneapolis, MN: Lerner Publications Co., 2003.

Videos

Eyewitness: Butterfly and Moth, DK.

The Magic School Bus: Butterflies!, KidVision.

Web Sites

All About Butterflies
http://www.enchantedlearning.com/subjects/butterfly/
Kidzone Facts for Kids
http://www.kidzone.ws/animals/monarch_butterfly.htm
Smithsonian National Zoological Park
http://nationalzoo.si.edu

About the Author

Dana Meachen Rau is an author, editor, and illustrator. A graduate of Trinity College in Hartford, Connecticut, she has written more than one hundred books for children, including nonfiction, biographies, early readers, and historical fiction. She watches the butterflies on the flowers in her garden in Burlington, Connecticut.

About the Reading Consultant

Nanci R. Vargus, Ed.D, wants all children to enjoy reading. She used to teach first grade. Now she works at the University of Indianapolis. Nanci helps young people become teachers. She also enjoys watching butterflies with her granddaughter, Charlotte.

Marshall Cavendish Benchmark
99 White Plains Road
Tarrytown, NY 10591-9001
www.marshallcavendish.us

All Internet sites were correct at the time of printing.

Library of Congress Cataloging-In-Data
Rau, Dana Meachen, 1971–
  The butterfly in the sky / by Dana Meachen Rau.
    p. cm. — (benchmark rebus)
Summary: "A rebus book that follows the lifecycle of a butterfly"—Provided by publisher.
Includes bibliographical references.
ISBN-13: 978-0-7614-2311-9
ISBN-10: 0-7614-2311-7
1. Butterflies—Life cycles—Juvenile literature. I. Title.
QL544.2.R38 2006
595.78'9—dc22
        2005026988

Editor: Christine Florie
Editorial Director: Michelle Bisson
Art Director: Anahid Hamparian
Series Designer: Virginia Pope

Photo research by Connie Gardner

Rebus images, with the exception of the pupa (pp. 10 and 12), provided courtesy of *Dorling Kindersley*.

Cover photo by *Photo Researchers, Inc.*/Stephen Dalton

The photographs in this book are used with permission and through the courtesy of:
Animals, Animals: p. 5 Donald Specker, p. 21 J.A.L. Cooke/OSF; *Dembinsky Photo Associates*: p. 7 Skip Moody, p.11 Gary Baker; *CORBIS*: p. 9 Joe McDonald, p.13 George D. Lepp, p.15 David Aubrey, p. 17 Richard Cummins, p.19 royalty-free.

Printed in Malaysia
1 3 5 6 4 2